"AROUND THE CIRCLE"

In 1892

ONE THOUSAND MILES by rail THROUGH THE Rocky Mountains.

Being a Descriptive of a Trip AMONG PEAKS, OVER PASSES AND THROUGH CANONS OF COLORADO.

A Journey which comprises more Noted and Magnificent Scenery than is compassed in any other one Thousand Miles of Travel in the known World

PRESENTED BY THE

PASSENGER · DEPARTMENT OF THE DENVER · & RIO · GRANDE R·R·

1892

BY S.K. HOOPER, GEN. PASS. AGENT, DENVER, COLORADO

EDITOR'S PREFACE

Colorado has long been a tourist state, and so guides to its peaks, valleys, rivers, canyons, and gold camps have had a long and plentiful history. In *Around the Circle* is a descriptive orientation to seeing the wonderlands by rail. The edition we reprint here appeared in 1892, and it was followed by many more on almost a yearly basis until automobiling became popular.

It was the aim of the Denver & Rio Grande Railroad to promote passenger travel on their scenic lines, and they were the original publishers and distributors of this introduction to "A Thousand Miles Through the Rocky Mountains." And there must have been something basically enduring about the allure of the Rockies by rail, for in spite of modern highways that have largely replaced the early steel net, several railroads still operate for tourists—as well as for natives. These penetrate some of the state's wildest and most scenic gorges and passes, and remain quite popular in the summer months.

This little guide in reprint form will thus serve not only as a nostalgic trip into the past but also as good background reading for the presently operating passenger lines. Railroad buffs from the casual to the serious will also enjoy this glimpse of real history. Surely, it will help all Americans appreciate even more the crest of their continent and their natural and pioneer heritage.

William R. Jones

INTRODUCTION.

HE TOURIST in search of grand and beautiful scenery finds an embarrassment of riches in Colorado. Among so many attractions he is at a loss which to choose, and having made a choice, he is frequently troubled with doubts as to the wisdom of his selection. Recognizing this fact, the Passenger Department of the Denver & Rio Grande Railroad, after a careful and thoughtful discussion of the situation, has decided to make a selection of a tour that shall embrace the most varied and picturesque scenery to be found on the line of any railroad in the world, included in a single trip, at a moderate cost. The excursion " Around the Circle " presents all these advantages. It can be made comfortably in four days, and no portion of the journey has to be retraced, thus affording constant variety and keeping the interest of the tourist pleasurably excited to the end. It is a remarkable fact that this journey, if pursued in the line laid down in the following pages, is cumulative in its character. Like a well-constructed drama, the interest grows stronger and stronger with each stage of its progress, until the final scene, which is an overpowering climax of grandeur and majesty. The points of interest on the trip " Around the Circle " are practically innumerable. The observing tourist will discover many beauties and attractions which are not described by the writer. No attempt has been made to include all that is worthy of mention. Only those scenes which are of transcendent interest have been touched upon, and in the pages which follow, the reader will only obtain a bird's-eye view of the tour. This being the case, the tourist can readily imagine what pleasure lies before him. In this instance distance does not lend enchantment to the view. To penetrate the heart of the majestic mountains, to cross and re-cross the great Rocky Range, to gaze with breathless awe into the defiles of abysmal chasms, and to behold with reverent, upturned eyes the ancient summits of heaven-defying snow-crowned peaks, are privileges that familiarity can never make commonplace nor belittle. Such privileges are granted to the tourists " Around the Circle," and with full confidence that he who takes the journey will find his brightest anticipations more than realized, this little book is placed before him.

SEVEN FALLS—CHEYENNE CANON.

"AROUND THE CIRCLE."

HE journey "Around the Circle" on the Denver and Rio Grande Railroad, from Denver to Silverton, Silverton to Ouray, and return to Denver, or via the Denver & Rio Grande to Durango, thence over the Rio Grande Southern R. R. to Ridgway and return to Denver, briefly described in the following pages, comprises more noted and magnificent scenery than any other trip of similar length in the known world. Piercing the heart of the Rocky Mountains, crossing and recrossing the "Great Divide" between the Atlantic and Pacific slopes ; penetrating five cañons, each of which is a world's wonder, and no two having the same characteristics ; climbing four mountain passes by rail and one by stage ; achieving grades of 211 feet to the mile ; reaching heights 11,000 feet above the sea ; penetrating gorges whose walls soar a half mile in perpendicular cliffs above the track ; traversing fertile and picturesque valleys, watered by historic rivers ; passing through Indian reservations and in sight of frontier cantonments of National troops ; pausing in the midst of mining camps, where gold and silver and coal and copper are being taken from subterranean recesses ; in a word, making the traveler familiar with peaks and plains, lakes and rivers, cañons and passes, mountains and mesas ; with strange scenes in nature, aboriginal types of men, wonders of science and novel forms of art ; surely no other journey of a thousand miles can so instruct, entertain, entrance and thrill the traveler as this trip " Around the Circle."

Every mile of the journey has its especial attraction. A thousand objects of interest present themselves to view in rapid succession. A thousand novel impressions photograph themselves upon the mind, a thousand landscapes of wonderful and bewitching beauty beyond the power of pen or pencil, or brush or camera to depict, can be seen from the windows of the car. Colorado is a land of wonders, a land of surprises, a land of sharp and wonderful contrasts. Take Toltec Gorge as a central point, and with a radius of two hundred miles describe a circle. Within the confines of that magic ring will be found more grand and wonderful scenery accessible by rail than within any similar circle swept anywhere on the surface of the world! Pilgrimages are made across the seas to behold the beauties of some one famed object   The Via Mala

PALMER LAKE.

attracts one, Mount Blanc another, the Colosseum a third, and the tourist, after all his great expenditure of time and money, comes away with one impression.

It ought to be the fashion for Americans to see something of their own country before they rush across the ocean to gaze at the wonders of the Old World. It is a good omen that many Americans appreciate this fact and are turning their attention to the unsurpassed scenery of their native land. The "Via Mala" is dwarfed into insignificance when compared with the "Royal Gorge." The hundreds of peaks among the Rockies, reaching an altitude of over fourteen thousand feet, should compensate one for the solitary grandeur of "Mount Blanc," while the ruins of the "Cliff Dwellings" tell of a race older than that which built the "Colosseum."

It would be impossible within the pages allotted for this book to give an adequate description of even half the noteworthy things to be seen in a journey "Around the Circle." All that can be attempted is briefly to characterize a few of the most remarkable objects of interest, objects which deserve to rank with the greatest natural attractions of the world, and most of which have already become known as marvels, to behold which would amply repay a journey across the continent.

The trip naturally begins at Denver, the great railroad center of Colorado, and a city of more than ordinary attractiveness.

For a hundred and twenty miles the railroad extending to the south follows the front range of the Rocky Mountains, which is in plain view on the right and to the west. After Denver has been left behind, the tourist can see from the car window the snow-covered pinnacles of Long's, James', Gray's and Pike's Peaks standing in a wilderness of lesser mountains. Soon a remarkable promontory rising from the summit of a conical hill and presenting the appearance of an ancient round tower, attracts the tourist's attention. This is Castle Rock, under whose battlements nestles a picturesque village of the same name. Beyond Castle Rock the country becomes more broken, the ascent being now begun at what is known as the Divide, a range of hills extending eastward into the plains and rising to an elevation of 7,500 feet. Curious formations of sandstone frequently occur, the most notable of which is called Casa Blanca, and can be seen on the right between Greenland station and Palmer Lake. This enormous monolith is a thousand feet in length and two hundred feet high, and on account of its size, its snow-white walls and its castellated appearance, can hardly fail to attract attention. On the summit of the Divide is Palmer Lake, a lovely little sheet of water, so equally poised that its waters flow through outlets northward into the Platte and southward into the Arkansas. Here has been established a pleasant summer resort, and here also is Glen Park, where assemblies are

CENTRE OF PIKE'S PEAK.

held each summer, modeled on those of the well-known Chautauqua. Beyond Palmer Lake, on both sides of the track, may be seen wonderful formations of brilliant red sandstone, taking the form of castles, fortifications and towers. One of the most striking of these has been named Phœbe's Arch, being a great castle-like upthrust of glowing red rock, through which there is a perfect natural archway. The descent of the Divide to Colorado Springs is through an interesting country, the mountains to the west and plains extending to the east. As Colorado Springs are approached, the great gateway to the Garden of the Gods can be seen to the right, and Pike's Peak, rising to an altitude of 14,147 feet, its summit white with snow, attracts instant attention. A side trip can here be taken, at nominal expense, to Manitou Springs, five miles distant, the famous watering place of the west, a pleasure resort possessing wonderful effervescent and medicinal springs, and surrounded by more objects of scenic interest than any resort of a like character in the old or new world, including " Garden of the Gods," " Glen Eyre," " Red Rock Cañon," " Crystal Park," " Ruxton's Glen," " William's Cañon," " Manitou Grand Caverns," " Cave of the Winds," " Ute Pass," " Rainbow Falls," " Bear Creek Cañon," " Cheyenne Mountain," " Pike's Peak," and hundreds of others, to name which space is lacking.

The cogwheel railroad to the summit of Pike's Peak is now completed and in operation, and is the most novel railway in the world. When it reaches its objective point above the clouds, at a height of 14,147 feet above sea level, it renders almost insignificant by comparison the famous cogway up Mount Washington, and the inclined railway up the Rhigi in Switzerland.

The route is the most direct possible, and about nine miles in length. The track is the same as that of the Mount Washington line, standard gauge, with an eight-inch cast-steel cog rail. The cars are set on low trucks to prevent them from becoming top-heavy on curves or in a high wind. This is almost an unnecessary precaution, as it is not expected to make the ascent in less than two hours. On the ascent the cars are pushed by the engine, but on the descent the locomotive is placed in front. The engine achieves the tremendous grades by means of a cog wheel, which fits into the cog rail. This mountain road is a great attraction, added to the many which already render Manitou the greatest summer resort of the mid-continental region.

The run from Colorado Springs to Pueblo is down the valley of a pretty little stream, the Fountaine qui Bouille, along whose banks are situated rich farms, or as they are universally termed in the west, "ranches," on which large crops are grown through the medium of irrigation. A hundred miles to the westward may be seen the faint blue outlines of the Greenhorn range of mountains, while to the eastward stretch the plains, the view of which is limited only by the horizon. Pueblo is the great manufacturing city of cen-

VETA PASS.

tral Colorado. It has one of the largest steel manufactories in the world, and a number of extensive smelters. Its close proximity to coal and iron mines, and the fact that it has become a railroad center of much importance, makes the future of the city exceedingly bright in promise. With a population of over 20,000, constantly increasing, and with the energy and push of its citizens, it cannot fail of achieving the greatest prosperity.

From Pueblo, 120 miles distant from Denver, the journey is continued to the south, still across a level country, and to the left the Spanish peaks soon rise to view. These mountains possess a peculiar attraction, rising, as they do, directly from the plain in symmetrical, conical outlines. and reaching an altitude respectively of 13,620 and 12,720 feet. The Indians, with a touch of instinctive poetry, named these mountains " Wahatoya," or Twin Breasts.

Shortly after sighting the Spanish Peaks, the ascent of Veta Pass is begun. The ascent of this famous pass is one of the great engineering achievements of the Denver & Rio Grande Railroad. The line follows the ravine formed by a little stream, La Veta Mountain rising to the right. At the head of this gulch is the wonderful " Mule-Shoe Curve," the sharpest curve of the kind known in railroad engineering. In the center of the bend is a bridge, and the sparkling waters of the mountain stream can be seen flashing and foaming in their rocky bed below. Standing on the rear platform of the Pullman car as the train rounds the curve, the tourist can see the fireman and engineer attending to their duties. From this point the ascent of Dump Mountain begins, rocks and precipitous escarpments of shaley soil to the right and perpendicular cliffs and chasms to the left. The ascent is slowly made, two great Mogul engines urging their iron sinews to the giant task. The view to the eastward is one of great extent and magnificence. The plains stretch onward to the dim horizon line like a gently undulating ocean, from which rise the twin cones of " Wahatoya," strangely fascinating in their symmetrical beauty. At the summit of the pass the railroad reaches an elevation of 9,393 feet above the sea.

Veta Mountain is to the right. as the ascent of the pass is made, and rises with smooth sides and splintered pinnacles to a height of 11,176 feet above the sea level. The stupendous proportions of this mountain, the illimitable expanse of planes, the symmetrical cones of the Spanish Peaks, present a picture upon which it is a never-ceasing delight for the eye to dwell. The train rolls steadily forward on its winding course, at last reaching the apex, glides into the timber and halts at the handsome stone station over 9,000 feet above the level of the distant sea. The downward journey is past Sierra Blanca and old Fort Garland, and through that pastoral and picturesque valley known as San Luis Park.

At Placer one can say that the descent of Veta Pass has been accom-

WAGON-WHEEL GAP.

plished, though it is still all down grade to Alamosa. This little town is situated on the eastern border of the San Luis Valley and at the western extremity of La Veta Pass.

From Alamosa station a magnificent view of Blanca is obtained, and this majestic mountain, with its triple peaks capped with snow, and two-thirds of its height above timber line, presents a noble and impressive spectacle. To the north and south, silhouetted against a sky of perfect azure, are the serrated pinnacles of the Sangre de Christo range. It would be difficult to find, even in this land of peaks, a more impressive mountain view than that obtained during the traversing of the San Luis Valley, on the eastern rim of which Garland Station, the site of old Fort Garland, rests. Here is a park 7,500 feet above sea level, surrounded on all sides by ranges of rugged mountains whose summits are whitened with perpetual snow. San Luis Park has an area larger than Connecticut, watered plentifully by mountain streams and traversed by the historic and beautiful Rio Grande del Norte. The soil of this valley is fertile, and through the medium of irrigation the park is rapidly becoming a great agricultural region.

From Pueblo the line diverges and the tourist may go via Veta Pass as described above, or to Salida, and thence through the Poncha Pass to Villa Grove and down through the beautiful San Luis Valley to Alamosa, noted for its fine farms and phenomenal yield of agricultural products. From the point named above there is a tangent of fifty-two miles and the San Luis Valley portion is a straight line through one of the most fruitful and beautiful sections of the State.

From Alamosa a delightful side trip can be taken to the Hot Springs at Wagon Wheel Gap, and to the new and already famous mining camp, Creede, for which a reduced rate will be given. A word about this wonderful health and pleasure resort will not be out of place here. As the Gap is approached the valley narrows until the river is hemmed in between massive walls of solid rock which rise to such a height on either side as to throw the passage into twilight shadow. The river rushes roaring down over gleaming gravel or precipitous ledges. Progressing, the scene becomes wilder and more romantic, until at last the waters of the Rio Grande pour through a cleft in the rocks just wide enough to allow the construction of a road along the river's edge. On the right, as one enters, tower cliffs to a tremendous height, suggestive in their appearance of the Palisades of the Hudson. On the left rises the round shoulder of a massive mountain. The vast wall is unbroken for more than half a mile, its crest presenting an almost unserrated sky line. Once through the Gap, the traveler, looking toward the south, sees a valley encroached upon and surrounded by hills

"Bathed in the tenderest purple of distance,
Tinted and shadowed by pencils of air."

SOUTH WILLOW CANON, CREEDE, COLO.

Here is an old stage station, a primitive and picturesque structure of hewn logs, made cool and inviting by wide-roofed verandahs. Not a hundred feet away rolls the Rio Grande river, swarming with trout. A drive of a mile along a winding road, each turn in which reveals new scenic beauties, brings the tourist to the famous springs. The medicinal qualities of the waters, both of the cold and hot springs, have been thoroughly tested and proved equal, if not superior, to the Hot Springs of Arkansas.

Ten miles beyond Wagon Wheel Gap is Creede; nothing yesterday, a city of seven thousand people to-day. Here is Colorado's newest and richest mining camp, bustling with all the activity of an older eastern city. Situated in the heart of a cañon and extending through it and widening out on to the less precipitous hills below, composed of buildings of all kinds, from the temporary "shack" of the prospector to the more pretentious brick store. The mountain side dotted with innumerable prospect holes, with an occasional large building of unpainted pine, rising from which is a volume of steam and smoke giving ocular evidence of the presence of a mine of more than ordinary interest and value. To the tourist desiring to combine business with pleasure, here is the opportunity to buy what at present seems only "a hole in the ground," but which may some day develop into a mint within itself.

Leaving Alamosa and continuing the circle tour, after crossing San Luis Park, and just before reaching Toltec Tunnel, a sharp curve takes the train into a nook among the hills. To the left are great monumental and fantastic forms of rock, while to the right are cliffs rising to a height of five or six hundred feet above the track. From the quaint and curious formations which rise to the left as this bend is rounded, it has been named Phantom Curve. In half an hour Toltec Tunnel is reached, the great peculiarity of which is that it pierces the top of a mountain instead of its base. For six hundred feet it has been blasted through the living rock, and such is its solidity that no masonry is needed to support the superincumbent rock masses above. When the train emerges from the tunnel it rolls out upon a bridge of trestlework set like a balcony against the wall of stone. Beneath, to the left, is Toltec Gorge. The traveler looks down fifteen hundred feet and, glancing upward, sees the opposite wall of the gorge rising a thousand feet above him. The scene is one of the most thrilling and unique in the whole journey " Around the Circle." Below, at the bottom of the gorge, swirls and dashes a little stream, whose waters are churned into snow-white foam, and the noise of whose progress comes faintly to the ear, borne upward from those tremendous depths.

An object of interest to all visitors to Toltec Gorge is the Garfield Memorial, a beautiful monument of granite, raised by the National Association of

RIO LAS ANIMAS CANON.

General Passenger Agents, who held service at this spot on the 26th day of September, 1881, at the time President Garfield was being buried at Cleveland, Ohio.

At Cumbres, the summit of the Cumbres range of mountains, is reached an elevation of 10,115 feet, and the journey of the descent is a trip fraught with great variety of scenery and abounding in interest. Here may be seen mountain meadows lush with vegetation, the surrounding hills being heavily timbered and abounding in game.

At Ignacio the Indian reservation is entered, and the rude tepees of the Southern Utes can be seen pitched along the banks of the Rio de las Florida. Occasionally a glimpse can be caught of a stolid brave, tricked out in all his savage finery, gazing fixedly at the train as it speeds by. Frequently there is quite a little group of these aborigines at the station, and they are always ready to exchange bows and arrows, trophies of the chase, or specimens of their rude handiwork in return for very hard cash.

From Durango the tourist has the choice of two routes to complete the "Circle" tour; either via the Rio Grande Southern Railroad, through the Mancos Valley, the Lost Cañon, the Valley of the Dolores and the Dolores Cañon to Rico, over the Lizard Head Pass by Trout Lake and Telluride, down the San Miguel and Leopard Creek to Ridgway ; or via the Denver & Rio Grande, through the Animas Cañon to Silverton, over the Rainbow Route (Silverton Railroad) to Ironton, and thence over the famous Ironton and Ouray Stage Road to Ouray.

RIO GRANDE SOUTHERN ROUTE.

Leaving Durango via the Rio Grande Southern line, the tourist is whisked across the Rio de Las Animas up Lightner Creek, past the silver and gold smelters with their seething furnaces and smoke and dust-begrimed workmen, and shortly past the famous coal banks where the black diamond is dug from the bowels of Mother Earth, and from there hauled to the smelters where it is used for the reduction and refining of its more exalted, but not more useful brethren.

Up through the valley the train speeds along among huge pines which thus far have escaped the woodman's axe, and which will be free from such invasion as long as Uncle Sam claims this particular spot as the especial reservation for the military post at old Fort Lewis.

From Fort Lewis the line passes through seemingly endless forests of pine trees, and after the reservation is passed an occasional saw-mill is sighted from its emitting unearthly screeches, which the knowing ones say is merely the head sawyer sharpening up. Descending the mountain into the valley,

CLIFF DWELLERS.

the beholder looks out on a broad expanse of fertile, well-watered country, surrounded on all sides by snow-capped mountains, and dotted with the rancheros of the hardy pioneer, who has been well repaid for his daring in locating in this far-away but beautiful valley, by its productiveness, and now that the railroad, that greatest of all civilizers, has come, he has abundant opportunities for the disposition of his produce.

In the center of this valley lies Mancos station, which is the junction with the main line of the proposed extension of this road into Arizona.

To the south of Mancos station, within a day's drive, and easily accessible, are the ruins of the strange habitations of an extinct and mysterious race known as the Cliff Dwellers. To those seeking curiosities and wonders, the great Cañon of the Mancos, the great Montezuma Valley, the McElmo Cañon, the Lower Animas Valley and the Chaco Cañon are the wonderlands of the world. They contain thousands of homes, and a town of the ancient race of Mound Builders and "Cliff Dwellers," that has attracted the curious ever since the discovery of America. The great Mancos Cañon contains hundreds of these homes which were built and occupied hundreds of years ago. Yet many of them are in a good state of preservation, and in them have been found hundreds of specimens of pottery, and implements of husbandry and warfare. This cañon is twenty miles south of Mancos, over a good wagon road. The cañon is cut through Mesa Verda, a distance of thirty miles, and the walls on either side rise to a perpendicular height of two thousand feet. These cliff dwellings are built in the sides of this cañon, as shown in the illustration. Fifteen miles farther west from the Mancos is situated the great Montezuma Valley, where thousands of fine specimens of pottery have been found among the ruins of that ancient people. On the west side of this valley is the great McElmo Cañon, also full of the ancient homes of the "Cliff Dwellers." Thirty-five miles south of Durango, in the valley of the Animas, are some extensive ruins of the Aztecs, and fifty miles further south are the wonderful ruins in the Cacho Cañon. These ancient Pueblos are, without doubt, the most extensive and the best preserved of any in the United States. Of these Prof. Hayden, in his report of the Geological Survey of the United States for the year 1866, says: " The great ruins in the Cacho Cañon are pre-eminently the finest examples of the works of the unknown builders to be found north of the seat of ancient Aztec Empire in Mexico." There are eleven extensive Pueblos in this cañon, nearly all in a good state of preservation, and their appearance indicates that they were once the home of fifteen hundred to three thousand people each. They are the most accessible from Mancos of any point on the line of railroads. From the thousands of ruins of cities, towns and families found throughout this great San Juan Valley, it is evident that once this great valley was the home of hundreds of

SULTAN MOUNTAIN.

thousands of this extinct race. That they were a peaceful and agricultural race of people is evidenced by the large number of their implements of husbandry and specimens of corn and beans found in these ruins, besides irrigating ditches and reservoirs for the storage of water.

Leaving Mancos, the road winds up the sloping sides of a flat-topped mountain, and there on its summit, among huge pines centuries old, bubbles up a clear, cold spring of sparkling water, forming the stream that flows down through the beautiful Lost Cañon, and is called by the unpoetic name of "Lost Cañon Creek."

Lost Cañon is a novelty in itself, as its sides are densely wooded and softly carpeted with a thick bed of moss and leaves, beautifully colored by millions of Colorado wild flowers whose delicate beauty is unrivaled.

Emerging from Lost Cañon the traveler is whirled up to the beautiful valley of the Dolores River, with its many ranches and farms, past the town of the same name. Off to the left, flowing to the eastward, comes bubbling down the mountain side into the larger river, the West Dolores, and no more famous or prolific trout stream exists than this.

Continuing on up the main river, the valley begins to narrow down, until we are once more within the walls of a cañon which takes its name from the stream flowing through it. While this cañon is not particularly deep, its natural beauties are manifold and are sure to make a lasting and delightful impression on the beholder.

Rushing out of the cañon the tourist is now landed at Rico. Rico is one of the most important mining towns of the State, whose mines dot the mountain sides, and whose product is packed in the cars on the backs of the ever-patient and faithful burro, without which no mining camp can be complete. The town is located in what was at one time the crater of a large volcano. Precipitous mountains with poetic names arise upon all sides of it, gradually widening, until by describing a circle of their summits they appear as the top of a huge funnel. Among them is the famous Telescope Mountain, a freak of nature only to be seen to form a proper realization of the aptness of its name. The place has much of historic interest, as evidences of early Spanish discoveries are found on many sides.

Leaving Rico, the line continues up the Dolores, which grows smaller and smaller, until it becomes a mere silver thread winding in and out among huge rocks and boulders. Thirteen miles north of Rico, and after climbing many miles of three and four per cent. grades, the summit of the Lizard Head Pass is reached at an elevation of nearly 11,000 feet. From the summit and to the left will be seen the Lizard Head, a peculiar rock formation capping a tall, bare mountain. This rock derives its name from its resemblaace to the head of a mountain lizard, though at the same time it may be said to resemble the shaft of some large monument.

OPHIR LOOP.

Descending the pass through the mountain gorges over rushing mountain streams, one finds one's self at Trout Lake. No more graphic description of this sheet of beautiful blue water can be given than a verse from a poem by " H. H."

> " The mountain's wall in the water;
> It looks like a great blue cup ;
> And the sky looks like another
> Turned over, bottom side up."

Here the sport-inclined tourist may spend a few days, for the lake is inhabited by thousands and thousands of mountain trout.

Shortly after leaving Trout Lake, the famous Ophir Loop is passed. Here the skill of the engineer was taxed to its utmost, for the track winds in zig-zags down the mountain side, rushing through a deep cut here, over a mountain torrent and a high bridge there, darting around sharp curves, in and out of snowsheds, until on the opposite mountain and high above us is to be seen a line of freshly-turned earth, which the knowing ones say is the track over which we have just passed.

From Vance Junction, a side trip of ten miles, which will well repay the tourist, can be made to Telluride, a mining town of some 2,500 inhabitants, nestling among snow-capped mountains, rising to stupendous heights and rich in gold and silver.

From Vance Junction the journey is continued down the San Miguel River, past Placerville, until the river leaves the rail, and again we commence to go up; this time over the Dallas Divide. This pass resembles Marshall Pass, though not quite so long. After reaching the summit, the line runs down the eastern slope along Leopard Creek, high above it on the moutain side, giving a most magnificent view of the Uncomphagre Range to the south with its gentle slopes softly colored by the deep, dark foliage of dense pine and fir forests, gradually rising until the mountains develop into a huge mass of shattered pinnacles, their topmost points covered with the everlasting snow.

Arriving at Ridgway, a city of some 1,500 inhabitants, the journey is again resumed on the original route via the Denver & Rio Grande.

THE RAINBOW ROUTE.

From Durango, the metropolis of the San Juan, to Silverton the scenery is of surpassing grandeur and beauty. The railroad follows up the course of the Animas River (to which the Spaniards gave the musical but melancholy title of " Rio de las Animas Perdidas," or River of Lost Souls), until the picturesque mining town of Silverton is reached. The valley of the Animas is traversed before the cañon is reached, and the traveler's eyes are delighted

ILLIUM CURVE.

with succeeding scenes of sylvan beauty. To the right is the river, beyond which rise the hills; to the left are mountains, increasing in rugged contour as the advance is made ; between the track and the river are cultivated fields and cosy farmhouses, while evidences of peace, prosperity and plenty are to be seen on every hand. Nine miles above Durango, Trimble Hot Springs are reached. The spacious hotel stands within a hundred yards of the road to the left of the track. Here are medicinal hot springs of great curative value, and here, in the season, gather invalids and pleasure seekers to drink the waters and enjoy the delights of this charming resort. Leaving the springs behind, the train speeds up the valley, which gradually narrows as the advance is made; the ascending grade becomes steeper, the hills close in, and soon the view is restricted to the rocky gorge within whose depths the raging waters of the Animas sway and swirl.

Animas Cañon has characteristics peculiarly its own. The railroad does not follow the bed of the stream, but clings to the cliffs midway of their height; and a glance from the car window gives one the impression of a view from a balloon. Below, a thousand feet, are the waters of the river—in places, white with foam; in quiet coves, green as ocean's depths. Above, five hundred feet, climb the combing cliffs, to which cling pines and hemlocks. The cañon here is a mere fissure in the mountain's heart, so narrow that one can easily toss a stone across and send it bounding down the side of the opposing rock wall until it falls into the waters of the river coursing through the abyss below. Emerging from this wonderful chasm, the bed of the gorge rises until the roadway is but a few feet above the level of the stream. The close, confining and towering walls of rock are replaced by mountains of supreme height. The Needles, which are among the most peculiar and striking of the Rockies, thrust their sharp and splintered peaks into the regions of eternal frost.

Elk Park is a quiet little nook in the midst of the range, with vistas of meadows and groves of pines, a spot which would furnish the artist many a subject for hiscanvass.

At the end of Elk Park stands Garfield Peak, lifting its summit a mile above the track. Beyond are marshaled the everlasting mountains, and through them for miles extends, in varying beauty and grandeur, the cañon of the Animas. Frequent waterfalls glitter in the sunlight, leaping from crag to crag, only to lose themselves at last in the onflowing river. Emerging finally from this environment of crowding cliffs, the train sweeps into Baker's Park and arrives at Silverton in the heart of the San Juan.

Silverton is interesting, both from its picturesque position and from the fact that it is a mining town. The mountains by which it is surrounded on all sides are honeycombed with the shafts and tunnels of innumerable mines.

MOUNT BEATLE.

Sultan Mountain, which overlooks the town, is a noble and impressive elevation, and adds to the grandeur of the scene by its regal presence.

From Silverton the journey "Around the Circle" is continued by taking the Silverton Railway, a road constructed up the difficult grades of Red Mountain, and doing an immense business in the handling of ores which are taken from these rich deposits ; also employed in the transportation of passengers. This wonderful road owes its construction to the genius, daring and wealth of one man, Mr. Otto Mears, who has for years been the "pathfinder" of the San Juan region, building toll roads and opening the gates of prosperity to the many mining towns of this mountainous country. He is the sole owner of the road, and has conquered engineering difficulties of the most astounding character. The line does not as yet bridge the gap between Silverton and Ouray, and from Ironton, its terminus, stages carry tourists over the mountains to the latter point, where the trip is resumed by the Denver & Rio Grande Railroad.

The stage ride forms one of the most attractive features of this most attractive journey. Lasting only two hours, passing over the summits of ranges and through the depths of cañons, the tourist will find this a welcome variation to his method of travel and a great relief and recreation. The old fashioned stage, with all its romantic associations, is rapidly becoming a thing of the past. A year or two more and it will have disappeared, except in rare instances, from Colorado. Here, in the midst of some of the grandest scenery on the continent, the blue sky above and the fresh, pure, exhilirating mountain air sending the blood bounding through one's veins, to clamber into a Concord coach and be whirled along a splendidly-constructed road, costing in some instances $40,000 a mile in its construction, to behold the grandest of Nature's handiwork, and to be in such close communion with the everlasting hills, is surely a novel and delightful experience.

The scenery on this journey between Silverton and Ouray is of the greatest magnificence. This is especially true of that portion of the route traversed by stage. The Silverton and Ouray toll road has long been noted for its attractions in the way of scenery, the triangular mass of Mount Abraham's towers to the left, while the road winds around the curves of the hills with the sinuosity of a mountain brook. The scene from the bridge over Bear Creek is one which once beheld can never be forgotten. Directly under the bridge plunges a cataract to a depth of 253 feet, forming a most noteworthy and impressive scene. The toll road passes through one of the greatest mining regions in the world, and the fame of Red Mountain is well deserved both from the number and richness of its mines. Before Ouray is reached, the road passes through Uncompahgre Cañon. Here the roadbed has been blasted from the solid rock wall of the gorge, and a scene similar in nature and rivaling in grandeur that of Animas Cañon is beheld.

MOUNT ABRAM, OURAY TOLL ROAD.

Ouray is one of the most beautifully situated towns to be found anywhere. Its scenery is idyllic. The village is cradled in a lovely valley surrounded by rugged mountains. The situation of the town is thus vividly described by Ernest Ingersoll in the "Crest of the Continent": "The valley in which the town is built is at an elevation of about 7,500 feet above the sea, and is pear-shaped, its greatest width being not more than half a mile, while its length is about twice that, down to the mouth of the cañon. Southward—that is, toward the heart of the main range—stand the two great peaks, Hardin and Hayden. Between is the deep gorge down which the Uncompahgre finds its way; but this is hidden from view by a ridge which walls in the town and cuts off all farther view from it in that direction, save where the triangular top of Mount Abram peers over. Westward are grouped a series of broken ledges, surmounted by greater and more rugged heights. Down between these and the western foot of Mt. Hayden struggles Cañon Creek to join the Uncompahgre, while Oak Creek leaps down a line of cataracts from a notch in the terraced heights through which the quadrangular head of White House Mountain becomes grandly discernible—the easternmost buttress of the wintry Sierra San Miguel.

" At the lower side of the basin, where the path of the river is beset with close cañon walls, the cliffs rise vertically from the level of the village, and bear their forest growth many hundreds of eet above. These mighty walls, two thousand feet high in some places, are of metamorphic rock, and their even stratification simulates courses of well-ordered masonry. Stained by iron, and probably also by magnese, they are a deep red maroon. This color does not lie uniformly, however, but is stonger in some layers than in others, so that the whole face of the cliff is banded horizontally in pale rust color, or dull crimson, or deep and opaque maroon. The western cliff is bare, but on the more frequent ledges of the eastern wall scattered spruces grow, and add to its attractiveness. Yet, as though Nature meant to teach that a bit of motion—a suggestion of glee was needed to relieve the somberness of utter immobility and grandeur, however shapely—she has led to the sunlight, by a crevice in the upper part of the eastern wall that we cannot see, a brisk torrent draining the snowfields of some distant plateau. This little stream, thus beguiled by the fair channel that led it through the spruce woods above, has no time to think of its fate, but is flung out over the sheer precipice eighty feet into the valley below. We see the white ghost of its descending, and always to our ears is murmured the voice of the Naiads who are taking the breathless plunge. Yet by what means the stream reaches that point from above cannot be seen, and the picture is that of a strong jet of water bursting from an orifice through the crimson wall, and falling into rainbow-arched mist and a tangle of grateful foliage that hides its further flowing."

CURRECANTI NEEDLE.

Resuming the railroad journey at Ouray, the traveler will find much to interest him in the run past Ridgway, where the Rio Grande Southern connects with the Denver & Rio Grande, to Montrose, where the main line is again reached, and, with faces turned once more to the eastward, the homeward segment of the " circle" is entered upon, and the greatest wonders of all this wonderful journey lie before. From Cerro Summit a fine view can be had of the Uncompahgre Valley, its river, and the distant peaks of the San Juan and Uncompahgre ranges of mountains. Cimarron Cañon is entered shortly after leaving Cerro Summit, the road following this cañon down Cimarron Creek to where it empties into the Gunnison river. Here begins the tourist's experience in the world-renowned Black Cañon of the Gunnison. The name is a misnomer. There is nothing black about the cañon except the shadows of the towering granite walls. The cliffs themselves show bright and happy colors. Gay contrasts of pink and blue, bright complements of red and maroon, all shades blended and differentiated, dashed on here and there as with the broad, free-handed sweep of some master scenic painter. The scene is varied, kaleidoscopic, constantly changing. Here the train rolls along between frowning and exalted walls ; there a stream of water, Chippeta Falls, white as wool, pitches from the brow of a precipice two thousand feet above ; yonder a side cañon yawns with capacious mouth as if to engulf us. Now we are in a spacious amphitheater, in the center of which stands a tremendous monument of solid stone, a spire graceful as if hewn by the hand of a Gothic builder, and terminating in a sky-piercing pinnacle. This is the famed " Currecanti Needle." Thus for twenty miles the ever-changing variety of the Black Cañon holds the awe-stricken attention of the traveler. At last the train rolls out into the valley of the Gunnison, and pastoral scenes take the place of the tumultuous grandeur just beheld.

But soon a new marvel demands attention. The ascent of Marshall Pass is just begun. We have just gone through the mountains, now we are to go over them. The Pacific slope is now to be achieved. Two powerful engines puff vigorously and take us spinning up the ringing grooves of this marvelous road, climbing grades of 211 feet to the mile with as much apparent ease as though we were traversing the level plain. What a varied panorama of mountain views meets the gaze, and when the summit is reached, 10,852 feet above the distant sea, the train pauses and the eye sweeps the prospect as far as vision reaches. To the right, fading away into the blue distance, can be seen the serrated range of the Sangre de Cristo Mountains, snow-covered pyramids of transcendent beauty. To the left towers fire-scarred Mount Ouray, a volcano whose fires died out ages ago, while opposite stands its companion peak, Mount Shaveno. Beneath is the pathway of our ascent, four lines in view, each one an ascending circle of our tortuous upward journey.

CATHEDRAL SPIRE.

Half a dozen revolutions of the wheels and we are on the Atlantic slope. The waters all run to the eastward now. One engine holds the train in check. There are no smoke and cinders. Pneumatic breaks skillfully applied by the engineer control the power of gravitation, which is the sole force needed to carry the long train down its winding way. The sinuosity of the descent is something indescribable. A glance at the illustration of the alignment of the road over Marshall Pass will convey a better idea than anything that could be said. The descent is ended at Poncha Springs, and the train enters the valley of the Arkansas.

At Poncha are some of the most remarkable hot springs to be found anywhere in the West. There are over one hundred of these springs; the water varies in temperature from 90 to 185 degrees Fahrenheit. The analysis of the Poncha Springs corresponds almost exactly with that of the waters of the Hot Springs in Arkansas.

From the Arkansas Valley can be obtained a fine view of the Collegiate range of mountains, including the peaks of Harvard, Yale and Princeton, all of which reach an altitude greater than fourteen thousand feet.

The crowning attraction, the wonder of wonders, the marvel of marvels, yet remains to be seen. The Grand Cañon of the Arkansas lies before us. There are no words in the language which can describe this cañon. There are no pigments on the artist's palette that can paint it; it is indescribable and entirely heyond the reach of mimetic art. The Grand Cañon is seven miles in length—seven miles of wonders, seven miles of the grandest, most awful scenery in the world. To the right boils and surges the Arkansas River, above which tower the red rocks of the cañon. To the left are cliffs, jutting in places above the track, and rising to tremendous and awe-inspiring heights. The progress down the cañon is by means of many intricate curves, and it seems as though the engine would dash itself to atoms against the cliffs, but each time a slight turn is made and the train rounds the promontory in safety. Soon the tourist finds himself in the heart of the mountain. Peak upon peak rises above him, until the splintered summits seem to touch the sky. Darker and darker grow the shadows, narrower and still more narrow grows the gorge, deeper and deeper grows the gloom, the river ceases its roaring, the noise of the train is hardly perceptible, for the engineer has "slowed up," and the Royal Gorge is at hand. Here the cañon is not wide enough for road and river, and here is one of the most remarkable feats of engineering. Right across the gorge, fifty feet wide at the base and perhaps seventy at the summit, which soars above to a height of nearly three thousand feet, a series of great iron braces has been thrown, from which huge iron bars depend, holding a long iron bridge in suspension, that clings to the face of the cliff, and runs, not across, but parallel with the course of the river. The eye

APPROACH TO THE BLACK CANON.

can scarcely comprehend the stupendous height of the perpendicular cliffs whose summits pierce the heavens half a mile above our heads.

After beholding the Royal Gorge the traveler has a superlative comparison for all that is wonderful and grand in nature. He has seen something which he can never forget, and of the many marvels of this marvelous journey "Around the Circle," the greatest of them all, the crowning glory, is the Royal Gorge.

It will not be inappropriate to make some special mention of several of the more important points of interest on the circle tour, and we add below a short description of the "Royal Gorge," "Toltec Gorge," "Animas Cañon," "Black Cañon of the Gunnison," and the "Marshall Pass."

THE BLACK CAÑON.

In all the world there is no place so beautiful, imposing, sublime and awful, that may be so easy and comfortably visited, as the Black Cañon, for the iron horse of the Denver & Rio Grande Railroad has a pathway through the cañon, and he draws after him coaches as handsome and pleasant as those which he draws on the level plain. Along many miles of this grand gorge the railroad lies upon a shelf that has been blasted in the solid walls of God's masonry; walls that stand sheer two thousand feet in height, and so close together that for most of the distance through the cañon only a streak of sky, sometimes in broad daylight, spangled with stars, is seen above.

> "I'll look no more;
> Lest my brain turn, and the deficient sight
> Topple down headlong."

Unlike many of the Colorado cañons, the scenery in this one is kaleido-scopic, ever changing. Here the train glides along between the close, regular and exalted walls, then suddenly it passes the mouth of another mighty cañon which looks as if it were a great gateway to an unroofed arcade leading from the pathway of some monstrous giant. Now, at a sharp turn, Chippeta Falls, a stream of liquid crystal, pitches from the top of the dizzy cliffs to the bosom of the sparkling river which dashes beside the road. Then a spacious amphitheater is passed, in the centre of which stands Currecanti Needle, solitary and alone, a towering monument of solid stone, which reaches to where it flaunts the clouds, like some great cathedral spire. Truly there is no gorge in all the Rocky range that presents such variety and grandeur as the Black Cañon of the Gunnison.

TOLTEC GORGE.

MARSHALL PASS.

Marshall Pass is entered almost imperceptibly from Poncha Pass, and the whole wonderful ascent might very readily be imagined as one and the same. The summit is almost eleven thousand feet above the sea, and the tortuous method by which the daring engineers of the Denver & Rio Grande Railroad have achieved this summit can best be understood by a glance at the cut illustrating the alignment of the track, shown on another page. As the train progresses up the steep the view becomes less obstructed by mountain sides and the eye roams over miles of cone-shaped summits. The timberless tops of towering ranges show him that he is among the heights and in a region familiar with the clouds. Then he beholds, stretching away to the left, the most perfect of all, the Sierras. The sunlight falls with a white, transfiguring radiance upon the snow-crowned spires of the Sangre de Cristo range. Their sharp and dazzling pyramids, which near at hand are clearly defined, extend to the southward until cloud and sky and snowy peak commingle and form a vague and bewildering vision. To the right towers the fire-scarred front of old Ouray, grand, solitary and forbidding. Ouray holds the pass, standing sentinel at the rocky gateway to the fertile Gunnison. Slowly the steeps are conquered, until at last the train halts upon the summit of the continental divide which separates the waters of the Atlantic and Pacific. The traveler looks down upon four lines of road, terrace beyond terrace, the last so far below as to be quite indistinct to view. Wonder at the triumphs of engineering skill is strangely mingled with the feelings of awe and admiration at the stupendous grandeur of the scene.

TOLTEC GORGE.

The approach to this great scenic wonder prepares the traveler for something extraordinary and spectacular. A black speck in the distance against the precipitous surface of a frowning cliff is beheld long before Toltec is reached, and is pointed out as the entrance to the tunnel, which is the gateway to the Gorge. As the advance is made around mountain spurs and deep ravines, glimpses are caught of profound depths and towering heights, the black speck widens into a yawning portcullis, and then the train, making a detour of four miles around a side cañon, plunges into the blackness of Toltec tunnel, which is remarkable in that it pierces the summit of the mountain

ANIMOS CANON AND NEEDLE MOUNTAIN.

instead of its base. Fifteen hundred feet of perpendicular descent would
take one to the bottom of the gorge, while the seared and wrinkled expanse
of the opposite wall confronts us, lifting its massive bulwarks high above us,

> " Fronting heaven's splendor,
> Strong and full and clear."

When the train emerges from the tunnel it is upon the brink of a
precipice. A solid bridge of trestle-work, set in the rock after the manner of
a balcony, supports the track, and from this coigne of vantage the traveler
beholds a most thrilling spectacle. The tremendous gorge, whose sides are
splintered rocks and monumental crags, and whose depths are filled with the
snow-white waters of a foaming torrent, lies beneath him, the blue sky above
him, and all around the majesty and mystery of the mountains.

ANIMAS CAÑON.

Animas Cañon is one of the wildest and most picturesque gorges in the
Rocky Mountains. Through it the Rio de las Animas Perdidas, or " River
of Lost Souls," finds its way to the valley below. For a dozen miles north of
Durango the Denver & Rio Grande Railroad traverses the fertile and cultivated valley of the Animas in its approach to the cañon. Soon the valley becomes more broken and contracted, the approaching walls grow more precipitous and the smooth meadows give place to stately pines and sighing
sycamores. The silvery Animas frets in its narrowing bed and breaks into
foam against the opposing boulders. The road climbs and clings to the rising
cliffs, and presently the earth and stately pines have receded and the train
rolls along a mere granite shelf in mid-air. Above, the vertical wall rises a
thousand feet ; below, hundreds of feet of perpendicular depth and a fathom-
less river. The cañon is here a mere rent in the mountain, so narrow one
may toss a pebble across, and the cramped stream has assumed the deep
emerald hue of the ocean. In the shadows of the rocks, all is solitary, and
weird, and awful. The startled traveler quickly loses all apprehension in the
wondrous beauty and grandeur of the scene, and, as successive curves repeat
and enhance the enchantment, nature asserts herself in ecstacy. Emerging
from the marvelous gorge, the bed of the cañon rapidly rises, until the roadway is but a few feet above the stream. Dark walls of rock are replaced with
clustering mountains of supreme height, whose abruptness defies the foot of
man, and The Needles, the most peculiar and striking of the Rockies, thrust
their splintered pinnacles into the region of perpetual snow.

ROYAL GORGE.

THE ROYAL GORGE.

The crowning wonder of this wonderful Denver & Rio Grande Railroad is the Royal Gorge. Situated between Cañon City and Salida, it is easy of access either from Denver or Pueblo. After the entrance to the cañon has been made, surprise and almost terror comes. The train rolls round a long curve close under a wall of black and banded granite, beside which the ponderous locomotive shrinks to a mere dot, as if swinging on some pivot in the heart of the mountain, or captured by a centripetal force that would never resign its grasp. Almost a whole circle is accomplished, and the grand amphitheatrical sweep of the wall shows no break in its zenith-cutting facade. Will the journey end here? Is it a mistake that this crevice goes through the range? Does not all this mad water gush from some powerful spring, or boil out of a subterranean channel impenetrable to us? No, it opens. Resisting centripetal, centrifugal force claims the train, and it breaks away at a tangent past the edge or around the corner of the great black wall which compelled its detour and that of the river before it. Now what glories of rock piling confront the wide-distended eye! How those sharp-edged cliffs, standing with upright heads that play a handball with the clouds, alternate with one another, so that first the right, then the left, then the right one beyond strike our view, each one half obscured by its fellow in front, each showing itself level browed with its comrades as we come even with it, each a score of hundreds of dizzy feet in height, rising perpendicularly from the water and the track, splintered atop into airy pinnacles, braced behind against the almost continental mass through which the chasm has been cleft. This is the Royal Gorge.

The following is a description of the points of interest in the exact order on the Trip Around the Circle, starting from Denver:

Castle Rock.—32 miles from Denver, east side of track. A bold and remarkable promontory rising from the plain.

Casa Blanca.—50 miles from Denver, between Greenland station and Palmer Lake, west side of track. An enormous white rock, 1,000 feet long and 200 feet high, presenting the appearance of a castle.

Palmer Lake.—52 miles from Denver. A beautiful sheet of water on the exact summit of the Divide, altitude 7,238 feet.

PIKE'S PEAK FROM THE GARDEN OF THE GODS.

Glen Park.—Half mile south of Palmer Lake, west side of track. Colorado's Chautauqua.

Phœbe's Arch.—One mile south of Palmer Lake, east side of track. A natural archway through a massive, castled rock of red sandstone.

Monument Park.—65 miles from Denver, distant view, west side of track, from Edgerton station. A natural park filled with fantastic and imitative rock formations.

Pike's Peak.—75 miles from Denver, 5 miles from Colorado Springs. The most famous peak of the Rockies, altitude 14,147 feet. Easy of ascent from Manitou.

Manitou Springs.—Manitou branch, 80 miles from Denver, 5 miles from Colorado Springs. The Saratoga of the West. Popular summer resort, wonderful effervescent and medicinal springs. Surrounded by more objects of interest than any other pleasure resort in the world, including " Garden of the Gods," " Glen Eyrie," " Red Rock Cañon," " Crystal Park," " Engleman's Cañon," "William's Cañon," " Manitou Grand Caverns," " Cave of the Winds," " Ute Pass," " Rainbow Falls," and " Bear Creek Cañon."

Garden of the Gods.—Manitou branch. One and one-half miles from Manitou. Famous the world over as a most interesting and wonderful park, abounding in strange and majestic rock forms.

Cheyenne Mountain.—Two miles south of Colorado Springs. One of the most beautiful of the Rocky Mountains, in which are the Cheyenne Cañons and the Seven Falls. Near the summit of this mountain is the burial place of the author and poet, " H. H."

Spanish Peaks.—Two twin peaks rising from the plains, without any foothills, forming a most striking picture. Visible all the way, to the eastward, from Pueblo until the descent of Veta Pass into the San Luis Valley is begun. Height of peaks respectively, 13,620 and 12,720 feet.

Sierra Blanca.—This monarch of all the Rocky Mountains, and the loftiest in the United States with but one exception, can be seen from Garland station, and remains in full view until the San Luis Park is left behind. Elevation, 14,464 feet.

Wagon Wheel Gap.—Del Norte branch. The hot springs of the Wagon Wheel Gap are famous for their curative qualities. The place is exceedingly picturesque and has become a favorite health and pleasure resort. The best trout fishing in the West. Distance from Denver, 310 miles. Elevation, 8,448 feet.

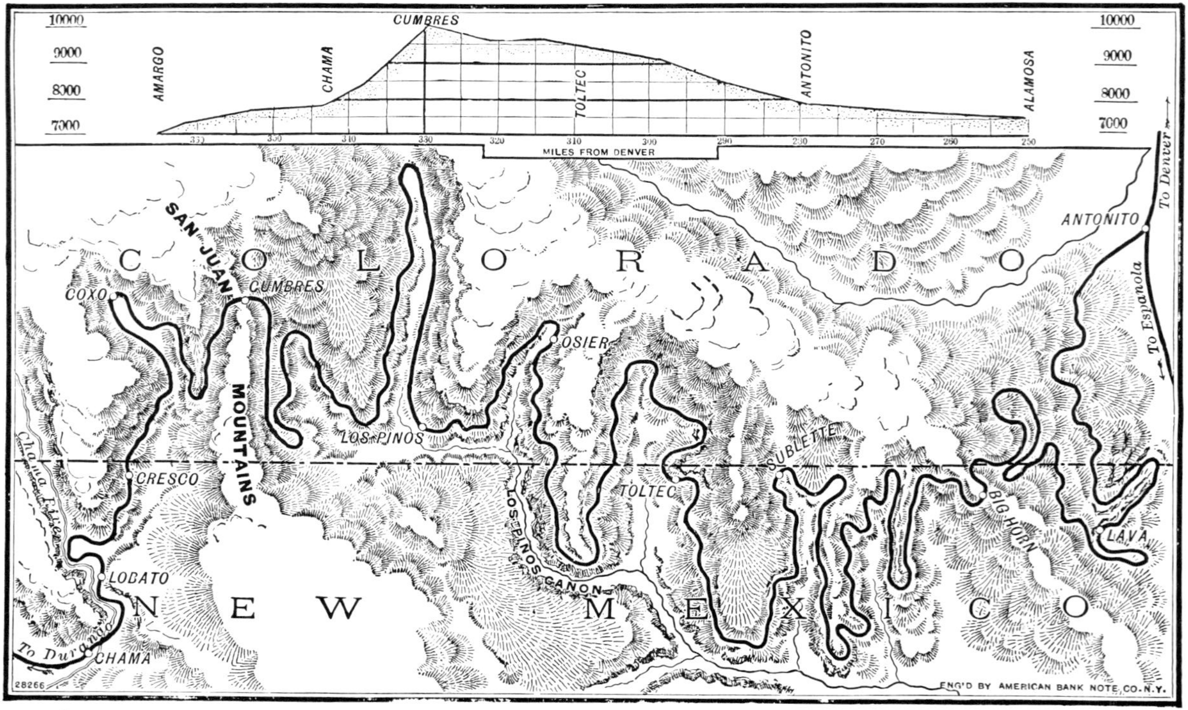

ALIGNMENT OF TOLTEC GORGE DISTRICT.

Creede.—Del Norte branch. New mining camp of great promise.
Population 8,000. The latest and greatest mineral discovery.

Entrance to the Gap.—Del Norte branch. The gap proper is a
cleft through a great hill with walls suggesting the palisades of the Hudson
and of about the same height. Through this gap flows the waters of the Rio
Grande del Norte, bright and sparkling, fresh from their mountain sources.

San Luis Park.—This park or valley is one hundred miles long by
sixty broad, altitude 7,000 feet, surrounded by mountains from 4,000 to 7,000
feet higher than the plain. The soil is fertile, and by irrigation is being de-
veloped into a fine agricultural region. Distance from Denver, 250 miles.

Phantom Curve.—After Sublette, 305 miles from Denver, has been
passed, the road makes a great bend around the side of a mountain ; on the
left rise tall monuments of sandstone cut by the elements into the form of
weird and fantastic figures ; this has been appropriately named " Phantom
Curve."

Toltec Gorge.—From Big Horn, distant 298 miles from Denver, to
Cumbres, there is a succession of magnificent and awe-inspiring views. About
midway between the two, at Toltec station, 309 miles from Denver, is Toltec
Gorge. The road traverses the verge of this great chasm, the bottom of
which is 1,500 feet below. The best view is on the bridge immediately after
passing through Toltec Tunnel.

Garfield Memorial.—Just beyond the bridge at Toltec Gorge stands
a monument of granite in memory of President Garfield. On the 26th day
of September, 1881, the National Association of General Passenger Agents,
at the time President Garfield was being buried in Cleveland, held memorial
services at the mouth of Toltec Tunnel, and since have erected this beautiful
monument in memory of the event.

Cumbres Summit.—Distant from Denver, 329 miles. Summit of the
Conejos range. Elevation, 10,014 feet.

Trimble Hot Springs.—Health and pleasure resort, 459 miles from
Denver, 9 miles from Durango and 36 miles from Silverton. The springs are
noted for their strong remedial character. Elevation, 6,644 feet.

Animas Canon.—Just beyond Rockwood, 469 miles from Denver, the
Animas Cañon begins. This gorge is formed by the breaking through the
range of the Rio de las Animas Perdidas. The road is built along a shelf cut
in the solid rock-wall of the cañon, which towers 500 feet above and drops
1,000 feet below the track. In this it differs from all other scenes on the line.

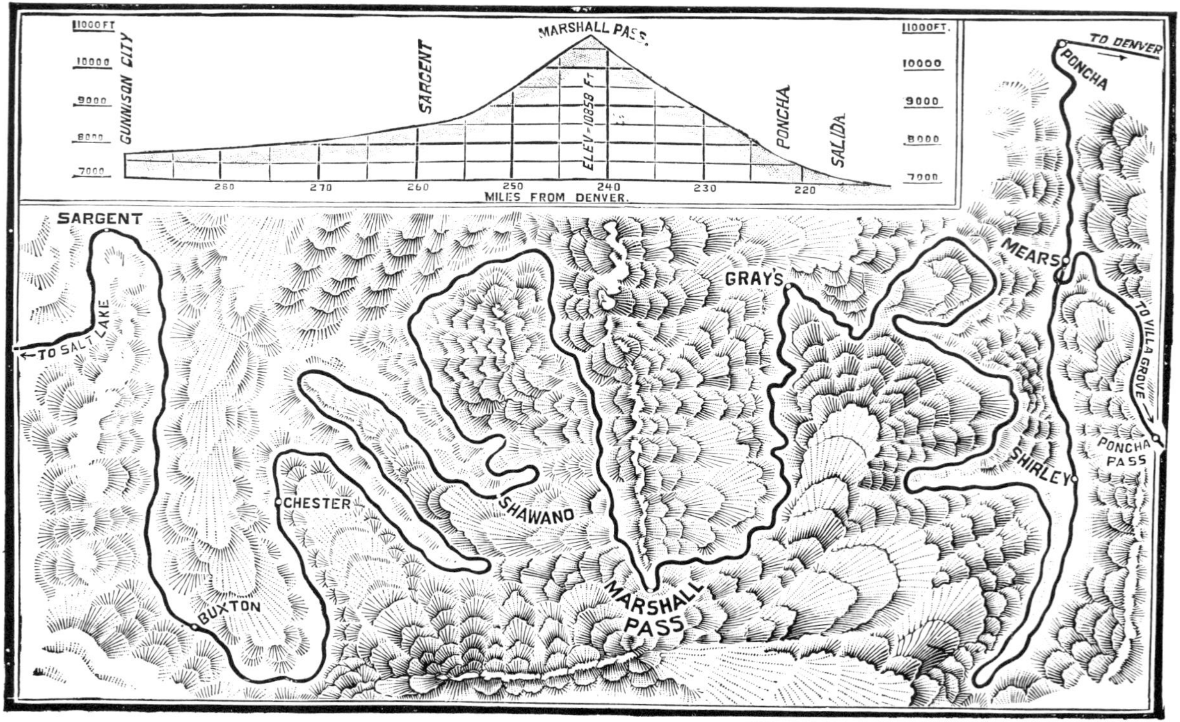

ALIGNMENT OF MARSHALL PASS DISTRICT.

The Needles.—After emerging from the western extremity of Animas Cañon, the traveler can see The Needle Mountains, the most peculiar and striking of the Rockies, thrusting their splintered pinnacles into the regions of perpetual snow.

Elk Park.—Animas Cañon having been passed, the road enters Elk Park, a beautiful little valley in the midst of the range, a spot rich in material for the artist in search of new impressions.

Garfield Peak.—At the western extremity of Elk Park rises Garfield Peak, a grand and impressive mountain towering to a height of a mile above the track.

Sultan Mountain.—Silverton, the terminus of this branch of the line, is 495 miles from Denver. It is surrounded by mountains rich in mineral-bearing mines. One of the most picturesque of these is Sultan Mountain, which reaches an elevation of 14,115 feet.

Ouray.—Picturesque mountain town. Hot springs of medicinal properties make this a resort for health and pleasure. The mines surrounding Ouray are among the richest in Colorado. Population, 3,000. Distance from Denver, 388 miles. Elevation, 7,640 feet.

Los Pinos Agency.—The ruins of the old Los Pinos Agency can be seen 13 miles from Montrose. The old store house and council chamber are still standing.

Cantonment of the Uncompahgre.—Nine miles from Montrose the road passes the Government post, where soldiers are still stationed.

Chippeta's Home.—Four miles from Montrose can still be seen the late residence of Chippeta, the widow of Ouray, the dead Ute chief, who was always the friend of the white man.

Uncompahgre Mountains.—After passing Montrose, 353 miles from Denver, a fine view of the Uncompahgre Mountains, extending to the southwest, can be obtained. Uncompahgre Peak, the monarch of the range, rises to an altitude of 14,235 feet.

Cerro Summit.—The ascent is commenced directly after leaving Cimarron station on the westward journey. From here the Uncompahgre Valley, its river and the distant, picturesque peaks of the San Juan are within full sight of the traveler.

Cimarron Canon.—Western entrance to Black Cañon, the road passing up Cimarron Creek, where it debouches in the Gunnison. The Cimarron abounds in trout and the country round about swarms with large game.

MANITOU.

Currecanti Needle.—Situated in a spacious amphitheater, midway of the Black Cañon, this curious monolith towers upward like a great cathedral spire.

Chippeta Falls.—A beautiful waterfall near the east end of Black Cañon, that plunges from the summit of the cañon wall, descending in a sheet of snowy spray to the Gunnison River below.

Black Canon.—Twenty-five miles west from Gunnison. Along many miles of this grand gorge the railroad lies upon a shelf hewn from the living rock, which rises frequently to an altitude of over two thousand feet. The cañon is sixteen miles in length, and abounds in many striking features.

Gunnison River and Valley.—Just after passing Gunnison City, 290 miles from Denver, the valley of the Gunnison is entered, and upon the right, as one journeys westward, flows the beautiful Gunnison river.

Mount Shavano.—Shavano is a companion to Mount Ouray, and rises on the opposite side of the track to an altitude of 14,238 feet.

Mount Ouray.—At the summit of Marshall Pass, 242 miles from Denver. An extinct volcano whose crater can be plainly seen. Altitude 14,043 feet.

Marshall Pass.—Begins six miles from Poncha Junction, at Mears Junction. The summit of the Pass has an altitude of 10,852 feet. From this point a magnificent view can be had of the Sangre de Cristo range extending to the southeast. The pass is a scenic and a scientific wonder, grades of 211 feet to the mile are frequent, and the ascent and descent are made by a series of most remarkable curves. The streams from the summit flow eastward into the Atlantic and westward into the Pacific.

Poncha Pass.—Two miles from Poncha Junction ; leads up to Marshall Pass.

Poncha Springs.—Five miles from Salida. Noted hot springs. Temperature of the water varies in the different springs, 100 in number, from 908 to 185° Fahrenheit. A great health resort. Altitude, 7,480 feet.

Arkansas River and Valley.—The railroad crosses the Arkansas River at Salida, and from the bridge, and until the town of Poncha Springs has been passed, a fine view can be had of the river and its fertile valley.

Collegiate Peaks.—Harvard, Yale and Princeton peaks, plainly seen from the vicinity of Salida to the northwest. Altitude, respectively, 14,383 feet, 14,101 feet, 14,199 feet.

BEAR CREEK FALLS.

Sangre de Cristo Range.—On approaching Salida, near the western end of the Grand Cañon, there is a break in the walls through which fine pictures of the Sangre de Cristo peaks present themselves.

The Royal Gorge.—The climax of all the grandeur of the Grand Cañon of the Arkansas lies midway in this wonderful chasm. The best view can be obtained from the famous hanging bridge. Here the walls of the cañon rise to a perpendicular height of 2,600 feet above the track.

Grand Canon of the Arkansas.—165 miles from Denver, between Cañon City and Parkdale, eight miles long. The world-famed chasm through which the river makes its way to the plains.

The following points of interest are located on the line of the Rio Grande Southern Railroad between Durango and Ridgway:

Cliff Dwellings.—Those interesting ruins are located in the Mancos Cañon and the Montezuma Valley, some twenty miles to the south of Mancos station, and easily accessible from that point by a delightful drive over a mountain road. A journey to this historic spot will well repay the time and trouble it would involve. Teams with guides and drivers can be engaged at Mancos.

Lost Canon.—This small cañon is between Mancos and Dolores, and though not so long or high as numbers of others in the Circle tour, is none the less interesting, as it possesses many novelties in the way of mountain scenery.

Dolores Canon.—While this cañon is not particularly deep, its natural beauties are manifold, and are sure to make a lasting impression on the beholder. This cañon is passed just before arriving at Rico.

Rico.—An important mining town of some 2,000 inhabitants beautifully situated in the center of a huge amphitheater of high, snow-capped mountains.

Lizard Head Pass.—A mountain pass similar to Marshall Pass, crossing the Uncompahgre Range at an elevation of 10,248 feet. The serpentine windings of the railroad up the mountain sides are full of interest.

Lizard Head.—A peculiar rock formation at the summit of the pass of the same name resembling the head of a mountain lizard.

Trout Lake.—A beautiful little lake of clear, cold mountain water, filled with thousands of trout. Good accommodations for the sportsman are near at hand, and a few days can be pleasantly spent here.

MOUNT OURAY, EAST SLOPE OF MARSHALL PASS.

The Ophir Loop.—The descent down the mountain side after leaving Trout Lake is called as above, and is one of the most daring and intricate pieces of railroad engineering that exists in the world.

Telluride.—Telluride is located on a branch from the main line some ten miles away. It is surrounded on all sides by high mountains whose faces are potted with innumerable mines, whose product is the chief source of revenue to the 2,500 inhabitants of this beautiful mountain town.

San Miguel River.—Leaving Vance Junction, the line follows the course of the San Miguel River through the beautiful Shenandoah Valley.

The Dallas Divide.—This divide is over a spur of the Uncompahgre Range on grades of three and four per cent. Leaving the summit, going eastward toward Ridgway and to the right of the train, is the main range of the Uncompahgre with its soft shaded sides towering into splintered pinnacles above.

Ridgway.—The northern terminus of the Rio Grande Southern Railroad and the junction of that road and the Denver & Rio Grande Railroad ; a city of some 1,500 inhabitants. Here are located the round-houses and the shops of the Rio Gr'nde Southern, giving employment to hundreds of machinists and laborers.

HEALTH AND PLEASURE RESORTS OF THE ROCKY MOUNTAINS.

Located on the Line of the Denver & Rio Grande Railroad.

On or Easily Reached from the "Around the Circle" Trip.

MINERAL SPRINGS.

Manitou Springs	Soda and iron.
Pueblo	Magnetic well.
Parnassus	Alkaline.
Carlile	Soda.
Cañon City	Soda.
Royal Gorge	Hot springs.
Wellsville	Hot springs.
Poncha	Hot springs.
Waunita	Hot springs.
Ouray	Hot springs.
Salt Lake City	Hot sulphur.
Buena Vista	Cottonwood hot springs.
Heywood	Hot springs.
Leadville	Soda springs.
Siloam Springs	Hot springs.
Steamboat Springs	Hot sulphur, iron and soda.
Glenwood Springs	Hot sulphur.
Wagon Wheel Gap	Hot springs.
Antelope Springs	Hot and cold.
Pagosa	Hot springs.
Ojo Caliente	Hot springs.
Trimble	Hot springs.

PLEASURE RESORTS.

Perry Park	Buena Vista	Ouray
Glen Park	Twin Lakes	Provo
Diana Park	Glenwood Springs	Lake Park
Manitou	La Veta	Cottonwood Lake
Beula	Palmer Lake	Evergreen Lakes
Salida	Monument Park	Steamboat Springs
Lake City	Colorado Springs	Wagon Wheel Gap
Cimarron	Cañon City	Trimble Springs
Salt Lake City	Poncha Springs	Antelope Springs
Trout Lake	Rico	Telluride

MOUNTAIN PEAKS AND PASSES OF COLORADO.

With Their Elevation Above Sea-Level.

	FEET.		FEET.		FEET.
Blanca	14,464	San Luis	14,100	Spanish	13,620, 12,720
Harvard	14,383	Red Cloud	14,092	Guyot	13,566
Massive	14,368	Wetterhorn	14,069	Trinchara	13,546
Gray's	14,341	Simpson	14,055	Kendall	13,542
Rosalie	14,340	Æolus	14,054	Buffalo	13,541
Torrey	14,336	Ouray	14,043	Arapahoe	13,520
Elbert	14,326	Stewart	14,032	Dunn	13,502
La Plata	14,302	Maroon	14,000	Bellevue	11,000
Lincoln	14,297	Cameron	14,000	Alpine Pass	13,550
Buckskin	14,296	Handie	13,997	Argentine Pass	13,100
Wilson	14,280	Capitol	13,992	Cochetopa Pass	10,032
Long's	14,271	Horseshoe	13,988	Hayden Pass	10,780
Quandary	14,269	Snowmass	13,961	Trout Creek Pass	9,346
Antero	14,245	Grizzly	13,956	Berthoud Pass	11,349
James	14,242	Pigeon	13,928	Marshall Pass	10,852
Shavano	14,238	Blane	13,905	Veta Pass	9,392
Uncompahgre	14,235	Frustum	13,883	Poncha Pass	8,945
Crestones	14,233	Pyramid	13,895	Tennessee Pass	10,418
Princeton	14,199	White Rock	13,847	Tarryall Pass	12,176
Mount Bross	14,185	Hague	13,832	Breckenridge Pass	9,490
Holy Cross	14,176	R. G. Pyramid	13,773	Cottonwood Pass	13,500
Baldy	14,176	Silver Heels	13,766	Fremont Pass	11,540
Sneffles	14,158	Hunchback	13,755	Mosquito Pass	13,700
Pike's	14,147	Rowter	13,750	Ute Pass	11,200
Castle	14,106	Homestake	13,687	Lizzro Head Pass	10,248
Yale	14,101	Ojo	13,640		

Seventy-two peaks between 13,500 and 14,300 feet in height are unnamed and not in this list.

ELEVATION OF LAKES.

	FEET.		FEET.		FEET.
Twin Lakes	9,367	Chicago Lakes	11,500	Palmer Lake	7,238
Grand Lake	8,153	Evergreen Lakes	10,500	Cottonwood Lake	7,700
Green Lakes	10,000	Seven Lakes	11,806	Trout Lake	9,800

ALTITUDE OF TOWNS AND CITIES.

Revised Since First Edition From Engineers' Measurements.

	FEET.		FEET.		FEET.
Alamosa	7,546	Ft. Garland	7,936	Pinos, Chama Summit	9,902
Animas City	6,554	Granite	8,945	Poncha Springs	7,480
Animas Forks	11,200	Grand Junction	4,583	Palmer Lake	7,238
Antonito	7,888	Gunnison	7,680	Pueblo	4,669
Aspen	7,775	Glenwood Springs	5,200	Red Cliff	8,671
Buena Vista	7,970	Howardsville	9,700	Rico	8,735
Cañon City	5,344	Irwin	10,500	Robinson	10,871
Castle Rock	6,220	Kokomo	10,631	Rosita	8,500
Colorado Springs	5,992	Lake City	8,550	Ruby Camp	10,500
Crested Butte	8,875	La Veta	7,024	Saguache	7,723
Conejos	7,880	Leadville	10,200	Salt Lake City	4,228
Cottonwood Springs	7,950	Las Pinos	9,637	Silver Cliff	7,816
Cuchara	5,943	Montrose	5,793	Silverton	9,224
Cumbres	10,015	Malta	9,580	Salida	7,050
Delta	4,963	Manitou	6,324	Telluride	8,758
Del Norte	7,880	Ojo Caliente	7,324	Trimble Springs	6,644
Denver	5,196	Ouray	7,640	Westcliffe	7,864
Durango	6,520	Ogden, Utah	4,286	Wagon Wheel Gap	8,448
El Moro	5,879	Pogosa Springs	7,108		

INFORMATION FOR TOURISTS.

Tickets will be placed on sale May 1, and continued until October 31.

Tickets for the journey " Around the Circle" will be sold for $28.00 from Denver, Colorado Springs, Manitou and Pueblo.

Tickets will be good thirty days from date of sale.

Stop-overs will be allowed at any point or points on the trip for any length of time within the life of the ticket.

Side trips can be taken to any point on the line, not covered by the round trip, at one-half the regular rates.

The purchaser can have choice of route, going either via Silverton and Ouray or Montrose and Ouray, or via the Rio Grande Southern R. R.

The journey " Around the Circle" can be comfortably made in four days, with rests at Durango, Silverton and Ouray. Or the entire thirty days can be profitably and pleasantly spent in viewing the wonderful scenery of the trip.